From VACATION RENTER to VACATION RENTAL OWNER

Everything You Need to Know about Vacation Rental Property Ownership, Management, Marketing, and Maintenance.

STEVE SCHWAB

ISBN: 978-1540306623

First Printing: August 2017

Published by 102nd Place LLC
Scottsdale, AZ 85266

Table of Contents

PREFACE

"Steve, it's not if things will go wrong, it's how you deal with them when they do."

Precious pearls of wisdom from my father. He taught me to appreciate the long-term value of a client and to do whatever it takes to make each client happy, even if that might mean losing a little money.

His advice has served me well over the years. Keeping my company focused on serving the vacation rental homeowner ethically and honestly has been a driving force behind my success.

Becoming the President and CEO of a major vacation rental property management firm was not originally in my plan. I graduated from college with a degree in criminal justice after having completed a tour of duty with the U.S. Army Reserves. I was fully prepared to enter the field of federal law enforcement but first I needed a break. I figured I'd take the summer off and then get serious about finding employment in the fall.

I packed up my stuff and headed to Rocky Point, aka Puerto Peñasco, Mexico. I'd been there before. It's a small town with friendly people, nice sandy beaches, and a laid back ambiance where I knew I could relax and refresh.

It didn't take long for me to settle in and pick up a few odd jobs, mainly bartending. I quickly became friends with many of the locals, including Cyndi, who would alter my future in the most dramatic way.

Cyndi was the owner of Cyndi's Beach Home Rentals. Her husband had recently passed away and she was having a difficult time running the business while trying to cope with her grief. She knew it was causing her to lose clients, but felt helpless to do anything about it.

One evening, when I was at the real estate office of my friend Jonni Francis, Cyndi happened to call. She told Jonni that she was ready to sell her business. Jonnie turned to me and said, "You'd probably be pretty good at that." *Really* I thought. At the time I had no experience in the hospitality industry but something about owning a business in this little piece of paradise appealed to me. The very next day I was in Cyndi's home going over the books. They weren't necessarily rosy but I felt that with a bit of hard work I could bring this company back. We signed the deal that day. Sea Side Reservations was born along with my career.

All of Cyndi's records were paper-based. She utilized no technology and everything seemed to be in disarray. Fortunately, I found the one piece of gold I needed – her old client list.

I immediately started making phone calls begging the owners to give me a chance. I promised that I'd do right by them – whatever it took to make them happy. Almost the entire list signed up. Now I just had to make good on my promise.

One of the lessons I learned early on, and had reinforced by Andy Ulrich, was that in order to be successful at anything you need to find people who have the strengths that you don't. In the case of a company you hire those people and then work as a team. Doing that one thing right changes everything. I was fortunate enough to find the right people quickly. In less than a year we were back on track; homeowners and guests alike were happy and the company grew.

About a year later, just before Christmas, I was coming home from a trip to the States and noticed several vans from Rocky Point Management (RPM) speeding past me in the opposite direction – strange. It didn't take long for me to learn that RPM was bankrupt. They'd taken the homeowners' rental funds that should have been in escrow and fled.

An HOA called to tell me that RPM hadn't paid the electric bills for any of their clients and the units were in danger of being turned off. I also learned that none of the RPM employees (maids, maintenance staff, etc.) had been paid. Many of the locals live paycheck to paycheck and with Christmas being just a few weeks away, I knew this would be a terrible hardship.

I tried to hire as many of the employees as I could. I took my own money and paid the electric bills so that owners wouldn't have the electricity turned off. I didn't yet have contact information for the former RPM owners but a few of them knew what I was doing. Word spread fast among the owners as they were so appreciative. Sea Side grew fast, proving once again that what you give comes back to you ten-fold.

Rocky Point Management taught me a huge lesson in what not to do. Never try to hide the worst. It only breeds contempt and worry about any future dealings.

While I had prided myself on being ethical and fair in all my interactions with both rental property owners and renters, I vowed from that point forward to have total transparency with our clients. I never wanted them to question what we were doing or why we were doing it. To meet that standard would take two things – better and more interactive technology and employees who understood and embraced my commitment to the homeowner.

Establishing the technology side was the easier of the two although not without some bumps along the way. Our original software developer was a company in China. When it became apparent that they wouldn't be able to keep up with our changing needs for a competitive edge, we parted ways.

Lucky for me a friend and competitor in the business, Carlos Corzo, had developed his own software system that he was willing to customize and sell to others. Carlos and I struck up a partnership and now all of our systems from booking to maintenance are state of the art. This includes a portal for the owners to see the status of their rental units 24/7 and even initiate their own maintenance projects if they like.

The employee side was more of a challenge. We were growing rapidly. It was no longer possible for me to speak with each new employee and impress upon them the vision and mission of our organization. In addition there were major cultural differences to be addressed between the employees (mainly Mexican) who spoke little or no English and the owners or renters (mainly Americans) who had different expectations.

Being sensitive to these cultural differences and finding effective ways to close the gaps has made me a better property manager. An example was our installation of "translator" software as a means to bridge the cultural gap. This way the staff could communicate in their native tongue, send it to an owner with photos, and have the owner receive a translated version in English.

We've also seen a significant impact from the institution of our ORANGE program. The program is designed specifically as a uniform way to express our culture putting the client first and foremost.

O – Owner Centric

R – Renters

A – Anticipate

N – Nurture

G – Guide

E – Excellence

Employees meet daily to review these tenets. They are involved and invested, frequently making suggestions to improve our processes for the benefit of the homeowner.

Our fledgling operation had grown to be the largest vacation rental property management company in Mexico by 2008. It was time to diversify. Like most destination spots, Mexico has a season – late spring, summer, and fall. Great money during the season but hard to make ends meet in Rocky Point come winter when no one is vacationing. Enter Scottsdale, Arizona – whose "season" just happens to be winter.

In 2009 we started Signature Vacation Rentals in Scottsdale with an eye to expanding to other vacation destinations within the U.S.; a great move that balanced revenue over the year and gave us a solid base for growth. Since then we've changed our name to Casago as we've expanded to become an international company.

As I said at the beginning of this story – I never planned to be a vacation rental property manager, but I'm so glad I took a risk and grabbed the opportunity when it came my way. I've learned so much in this process. I've learned that I love creating order out of chaos, that I love finding ways to solve challenges, that I love building websites and technology that drive the business for us and our clients. But most importantly, I've learned that I truly love working with people to ensure their needs are met and they have the best experience possible.

This passion is the main reason I decided to write this book. I've seen too many people be taken advantage of by unscrupulous property managers because they didn't know what they didn't know. It's one of the reasons that the industry hasn't always had a stellar reputation. I'd like to change that by giving you the information you need to make your vacation rental owner experience the best it can be.

In Part One we're going to explore what it means to become a vacation rental owner. We'll look at things like:

- Your goals in owning a vacation rental
- What location is right for you
- Market considerations
- Seasonality
- Understanding the risks
- Total costs of ownership

Part Two takes a look at the things you are personally responsible for as an owner. I'll talk about issues like insurance, Home Owners' Associations, safety and security, repairs and maintenance, and everyone's favorite topic – taxes.

Part Three delves into how you can set your guests' expectations so that what they see, or read, is what they get. Items such as ethical marketing, setting rates, taking reservations, contracts and legal issues will be discussed. I'll even give you the pros and cons of allowing pets. (Hint – I always say no.)

Part Four will give you the information you need to decide if you have the desire to manage the property yourself or hire a property manager to do it for you. And by manage I don't just mean taking care of the property – I'm talking about marketing, booking, collecting and paying transient taxes, along with a whole host of other issues in addition to maintaining the property in tip-top shape.

If you do decide to hire a property manager, I'll even give you the top ten questions you should ask them first.

Owning a vacation rental property can be a rewarding experience both personally and financially. You just need to be smart about how you go about it. Do the research. Make sure you go into it knowing everything you need to ensure it's a good fit for you. This book will help.

To your success!

Steve

PART ONE

BECOMING AN OWNER

SETTING GOALS

So you've just returned from your dream vacation: a perfect house in a perfect area with perfect weather. Everyone got along and the activities were amazing. More than once during your stay in paradise you thought about owning your own vacation home. How great to come back year after year to relive old memories and make new ones, to relax and let the stress of everyday life melt away. Would rental income help you afford it?

Or maybe you've owned a vacation home for several years, but you're finding that you just don't seem to use it as much as you used to. The kids are grown and have their own lives, while time spent visiting them takes up more of your travel budget leaving your vacation home empty. You don't want to sell it but you'd consider sharing it with others. Could the place earn its keep?

Or maybe you've got some cash you'd like to invest and you're thinking real estate is still a good market, but buying and flipping doesn't appeal to you. No, you're looking for a passive stream of income that will not only pay for the property but provide an excellent return as well. Is the answer in vacation rentals?

Whatever your reason for getting into the vacation rental property market, making a decision to rent your home means going into a business endeavor. Like any business, to be successful you need to understand your goals and what it is you want to achieve.

You may simply want to subsidize a portion of the expenses of owning your dream vacation home. You may want to cover all the expenses but still be able to enjoy the home on occasion. Or perhaps you have no interest in using the home yourself but view vacation rentals as a great investment opportunity. Once you're clear on why you want to rent your property, the next step is to determine your financial objective.

To do this you'll need to understand occupancy as well as rental rates in your area including the difference between seasonal and non-seasonal rates. You'll also need to have a grasp on the total cost of ownership – not just your mortgage but utilities, HOA fees, property taxes, etc.

For now, let's just keep it simple. Assume you have a mortgage of $2,000 per month and your goal is to subsidize the mortgage with rental income. We'll also assume that the "season" for your rental property runs 10 weeks and you can charge $2,000 per week during the season. Your off-season rate is $1,000 per week. To fully subsidize your mortgage you'd have to rent your home for all 10 seasonal weeks ($20,000) and 4 of the non-seasonal weeks ($4,000).

The calculations remain basically the same if you want to cover all of your costs or you want to earn income in addition to covering your costs. The reason you want to be clear about your financial objective is that it gives you a clear picture of how often, and more importantly when, you will be able to use your vacation home. If your financial objective is high, then you may not be able to use your home during the "season" because you'd be giving up the income that you need. Conversely, if your financial objective is low, you'll have more flexibility in when the home is available for personal use.

Total Cost of Ownership

Here's a brief list of some of the things you should consider when looking to cover your total cost of ownership with rental income:

1. Mortgage

2. HOA fees (Home Owners' Association)

3. Insurance (property and liability)

4. Property Taxes

5. Utilities

6. Garbage collection

7. Landscaping

8. Pool Service

9. Wear and tear (cost of items that will need to be replaced regularly i.e. linens, light bulbs)

10. Routine maintenance

11. Cleaning

12. Marketing and booking expense (if you do it yourself)

13. Property management fees (if you hire someone to do it for you)

14. Use taxes/transient taxes

15. Security systems

16. Internet/Cable

17. Rental permits

If you currently own your vacation property you already have a good feel for these costs but you'll need to do your research to determine what homes like yours are renting for.

If you are looking to buy a property you'll also need to do research on rental rates in your market. It will be important to have a feel for the potential total costs before making a decision to buy. Costs may vary by type of property selected so let's talk a bit about that.

<u>DIY or Hire Someone</u>

A key component of your personal and financial objectives will be determining exactly how you are going to manage the rental business. Are you going to do it yourself or will you hire a property management firm? Each of them comes with different costs and different time commitments from you.

The DIY versions may seem to be less expensive but to be successful you will need to spend a large amount of time marketing, booking, and maintaining your vacation home. On average a vacation rental owner spends 9 hours per week under normal circumstances. You'll also be on call 24/7 for any mishaps that may occur while your unit is rented. What is your time worth?

Hiring a property management firm seems to be a good choice for many people who don't have the time, the experience, or the inclination to take care of all the details that owning a vacation rental property entails. You'll get a better idea of everything that is required as you read further along in this book.

TYPES OF PROPERTY

Not every property makes a good rental. There are several factors for consideration, primarily location, which I discuss in more detail a bit later.

When considering property to buy with the intention of renting, stop, take a breath, and don't think only with your heart. Keep in mind that you have a financial, as well as a personal, objective in purchasing a vacation rental. While a rustic, one-room hut on the beach may appeal to your sense of romance, adventure and fun – it may not for the majority of the renters in your market.

To the extent possible you should try to take the emotion out of your purchase while still obtaining a property that meets your needs and will give you years of enjoyment. Look at the various properties and options offered. Adding an additional bedroom, an extra bath, a larger lot, or a higher or lower floor for a better view may have more rental income potential. There's a saying I coined for waterfront property views, "the more blue, the more green." Any additional cost incurred might be small compared to purchasing the wrong property.

Short-term vacation rental properties are generally condominiums, single-family, or multi-family homes. These homes can be located in resorts, on or near beaches, lakes, rivers, forests, deserts, or mountains, in urban or rural settings.

The style may be high-rise condominium, residential townhouse, single bedroom cottage, multi-bedroom homes, or a combination of mixed use lodges. To effectively compete for rental income with other properties in the area, the style of home you choose should reflect its surroundings.

A high-rise condominium with full service options or a single-family dwelling in the same area may both meet your personal needs.

The high-rise condo offers convenience with a small shop, weight room, community pool, laundry, café or restaurant, bar, and concierge. The single-family dwelling with multiple bedrooms, private pool, laundry, in-home theatre, and access to nearby shops and restaurants offers privacy.

While personal preference will be a key in determining what style of rental to buy, you may also want to take a look at your target market of renters. Who do you want to rent your unit to? How old are they? How much income do they earn? Are they single, married with no children, or families?

If your ideal renter is a family with young children, or a retired couple who likes to bring the grandchildren along, then a single-family dwelling might be perfect. However, if your ideal renter is a couple, or a foursome of golfers, then a full-service condominium might be better suited.

Knowing the demographics of your target market is important because that helps you determine the style of rental. But equally important is to know their psychographics. What do they like to do? Where do they like to do it? Who do they like to do it with? What makes them come to the market you're considering?

Is your property conducive to these types of renters? For example, if the main driver for renters in the location you're considering is snow skiing but your property is located ten miles away from the slopes, it's probably not going to be their first choice. Or maybe you want a home in Orlando – a big family vacation market. If the property only has one bedroom it may not be attractive.

Answering these questions helps you to determine the ideal location of your rental. And we all know when it comes to real estate – location, location, location!

LOCATION

Ah yes, location, location, location – it's important for the resale value of your primary residence and equally important in the income potential of your vacation rental.

Where is it that renters like to go? What places attract the most people? What activities are readily available to entertain? How do those things mesh with your objectives for personal enjoyment of the property?

Some destinations that quickly come to mind would be beaches, lakes, rivers, ski areas, famous golf courses, and major attractions like Disney Land just to name a few. A snowbird's destination might be to a warm, sunny beach in the winter while snow buffs may prefer the mountains of Colorado. Adventure seekers might like a cabin on an Alaskan lake while a golf enthusiast could go for a condo with a view of the 18th hole at a signature course. Singles or couples without children might be looking for a destination with a vibrant nightlife while families could be content with outdoor activities like biking and hiking.

Because you've spent time determining your goals and objectives, it should be easy for you to determine what destination(s) best fit your vacation needs as well as those of your target market. But just because you know where, doesn't mean you should rush into purchasing a property.

There are many things you should take into account first. Make sure you research the following areas before making a final decision on a place: market considerations, amenities, and seasonality. The concept of seasonality is important so I'm devoting an entire chapter to it later on. For now, let's discuss the other two.

<u>Market Considerations</u>

While it may be true that any rental property in a "destination" location has income potential, the actual amount of that income will be positively or negatively impacted by the market.

Your first step should be to determine the economic situation and future for the area. Is it booming even when not "in season?" Are jobs being created or are they leaving? Are more people moving in than are moving out? How many people are flying in to the nearest airport? Is tourism on the rise or the decline? Much of this information can be gleaned from the local area Chamber of Commerce.

But if you really want to get a feel for what's going on it pays to speak with the locals. Visit some bars, restaurants, and hotels in the area. Talk to the staff. Are they always busy? If not, when are they slow and how long does it last? Do the visitors tip well? What type of clientele does the area attract and why? Why do they choose to live and work here?

It is also important for you to know who you will be competing against for the renters' dollar and what exactly your competitors are offering. If there are a lot of resort hotels in your destination it behooves you to stay a night or two in some of the ones that are rated highly. What is it they are offering? Can you match or better a renter's experience with your property?

You should take into account the "price per person" when determining whether or not you have an advantage. For example, a family of six may have to rent two rooms in a resort hotel in order to have enough beds. Each room might cost $250 per night so a one week stay would cost roughly $583 per person. If your 3 bedroom condo is renting for $2500 per week then the cost per person is only $417. The renter saves 28% by staying with you.

The type of vacation rental property purchased should fit your long-term strategy. Purchasing the smallest possible vacation rental property in a thriving area just to have a place for your immediate family to enjoy is fine. But it may or may not be the best strategy for future income. I have seen owners of two-bedroom condominiums miss out on major rental income because their place was too small for the number of bedrooms renters needed.

In addition to size you should consider its uniqueness. A property that is unique may produce income regardless of size. For example, I purchased a four-bedroom condo in a beach community when two-bedrooms were popular among owners. In my due diligence I realized there were very few four-bedroom condominiums in the rental pool. I paid extra for the corner location giving me an additional 90° view from my upper floor patio. Guests could enjoy sunrise in the morning and a beautiful sunset in the evening from the comfort of my patio lounge chairs or even from the Jacuzzi. This gave me a distinct advantage in the rental pool.

You'll also want to explore the occupancy rates for not just the hotels in the area but other vacation rental properties as well. A real estate agent who specializes in vacation property or a reputable vacation rental property management company should be able to give you a good feel. They should also be able to provide some insight as to what types of units/homes rent well and which do not. If you've had your eye on a cute little one-bedroom bungalow but you learn the market is saturated with those types of rentals then you may increase your revenue potential by buying a multi-bedroom place instead.

Be creative in your thinking about where to locate your vacation rental. People rent for all kinds of reasons, not only for vacation. For example, a condo next to an active conference center or arena in a major city may have great rental potential. Something else to consider might be a rental property close to medical centers. Medical tourism is in demand in some areas. If you aren't familiar with the term, medical tourists are those who are coming to an area because they need to see some kind of specialist or have a specific procedure done that may not be available in their home market. Or they simply want the privacy of having their issue dealt with away from the prying eyes of friends or family.

Amenities

Once you've narrowed your search to a general location that meets your objectives it's time to start looking at specific properties. Knowing the kinds of amenities renters are looking for will impact the amount of rental income you can expect.

There are two types of amenities – internal and external. Internal are those things that are found inside the rental property. External amenities are the things which are found outside and/or near the rental property. For the purposes of this discussion on location I'm going to focus on the external amenities. I'll talk about internal amenities more in Part 3 – Setting Guest Expectations.

External amenities are those things that surround your home, for example: a pool, a spa, a barbeque pit, or a casita. Heated pools in particular can significantly affect the price and occupancy rate in "snowbird" markets. You'll want to check the direction the pool faces. A pool that has sun exposure will extend your season. A pool mostly in the shade will increase your cost to keep it heated to a comfortable temperature.

I want to bring up the concept of "view" here as it can be one of your primary external amenities. What will renters see when they look out the windows, lounge by the pool, or sit on the deck? Will it be mountains, trees, water, or the neighbor barbequing next door? Whatever the vacationer came to do is probably also what they came to see. So a skier in Colorado will pay more for a view of snowcapped mountains.

A beach lover in Florida will pay more for a view of the beach. You get the idea. It's always a good strategy to upgrade to the best view you can afford within your budget. And if you can't see it, at least be conveniently located to access it.

Also included with external amenities is the property's proximity to restaurants, bars, shopping, events, amusement parks, landmarks, beaches, fishing, or medical care facilities. The amenities offered in or near the property add to the potential enjoyment of your guests. The more of these you have, and the higher the quality, the more you can charge for your property. In fact, I've found that properties located near major attractions have the highest income potential because of the numbers of people drawn to these attractions.

The opposite is true if the property is located too close to things that renters might find negative. Some examples might be: proximity to overhead power lines, a garbage disposal site, major industrial sites, or even a beach with strong tidal activity or a rocky coastline.

A few years ago a well-known developer turned politician purchased a property in the Baja close to a nice green hill. The only problem was the nice green hill was actually a human waste processing site. Depending on wind direction the odor was unbearable. As you might expect the development failed.

Noise is often a major turnoff. Is the property you are considering near a train track, major highway or busy street, or in the flight plan of a nearby airport? How loud is the sound of the ocean crashing against the shore? All of these create noise that can be annoying to guests not accustomed to such surroundings.

I'm not saying that you shouldn't purchase a rental simply because there may be some negative issues. After all, an active noisy resort will be attractive to those individuals who are looking for a vibrant atmosphere. I am saying that it's important for you to do your due diligence and know exactly what you're purchasing both inside and out. Industry averages will tell you that about half of your vacation rental income will come from repeat renters. If the surrounding amenities are of a level that might deter repeat rentals then it may be best to keep looking.

The main question to ask is – do you love it yourself? Chances are if you do then others will too.

SEASONAL RENTALS HAVE A SEASON

Unless you're looking at a vacation rental that happens to be in a year-long vacation destination like New York City or the Hawaiian Islands you will be affected by the concept of seasonality. Once you've chosen a location, you have chosen a season. The longer the season, the better the income potential.

The first thing that pops into mind when thinking about seasonality is the premium rate you can charge to rent your property during the season. As a general rule of thumb, a week's worth of in-season rental is about equal to a month's worth of off-season rental. For example, if your property rents for $3000 per week during the season, you should expect to earn only $3000 per month in the off-season. So a longer season means you have the potential to generate more income from your property. And that can be a double-edged sword.

Most likely you're interested in the property because you vacationed at that destination during the season and enjoyed it. You'd like to do that again but now you understand that you'll be missing out on significant potential income if you do. Depending on your financial objectives the ability to use the property during the season may or may not adversely affect you.

If rental income is a key component to your ability to own and maintain the property then I recommend you visit the destination during the off-season before you buy. Does it still have the same appeal? Will you be able to enjoy yourselves just as much? Is the added income a reasonable tradeoff? If not, then perhaps owning a vacation rental at this destination may not be right for you.

Income however is only one consideration of seasonality. Weather, both in-season and off-season, can also play a significant role. It is important for you to understand what weather might mean to the cost of owning your vacation rental. It can affect upkeep and maintenance both inside and out.

On the exterior for example, a beach vacation rental may be susceptible to damage from salt in the air. Salt can be corrosive over time to air conditioning units as well as patio furniture, barbeques, cars and wiring – basically anything containing metal. Salt is also known to work its way into wood which may cause structural weakening over time.

If your vacation rental happens to be in a ski area, renters will be tracking in snow. This could have an adverse effect on the interior of your home. Melting snow can damage wood floors or ruin carpeting and so can the salt that might be traipsed in from roads and sidewalks.

Something else that can be affected by seasonality is wildlife and not just the four-legged variety. Insects, scorpions, and even birds can create maintenance issues. A Florida home on a golf course might require special screening around the pool to keep mosquitoes and other pests from bothering your guests. An Arizona home boasting wonderful desert mountain views might need a fence around the yard to keep coyotes and curious javalina from visiting.

None of these examples would be a reason to not purchase a vacation rental property. They are simply things that you should consider when calculating your total cost of ownership.

UNDERSTANDING THE RISKS

As I mentioned earlier in this book, once you've made the decision to turn your property into a vacation rental you have essentially started a business. And, as with any business, there are risks involved.

Vacancies

At the top of the list is the risk that no one will rent your home or that bookings don't live up to expectations. There are several factors that contribute to this, a few of which are:

1. Where, when and how you market.

2. The ease of your booking system.

3. The condition of your home in relation to how it is described.

4. How you handle problems when they arise.

5. Good or bad reviews.

6. Local laws or HOA restrictions.

Let's touch on marketing for a minute. These days the majority of vacation rentals are booked online. Your property needs to be accessible 24 hours a day, 7 days a week. If you're going to use your own website to market your property, how are you going to drive traffic to it? Do you have experience in writing good ad copy? Do the pictures of your home look professional?

If you decide to use a service like AirBnB or VRBO you'll stand a better chance of reaching potential renters – but only those who specifically access those sites. You will be responsible for writing the ad copy and getting your photographs uploaded.

A good property management company may be your best solution in terms of marketing. If they are leaders in the industry, like my company, they'll have access to marketing your property not only on all the self-service sites but also on the MLS, their own websites and multiple other options that may not be open to individuals. They should have experts in developing just the right words to sell your property, as well as professional photographers to show your property at its best.

Most people are pressed for time. They don't want to spend hours and hours trying to find and book a vacation rental. Your booking system must be easy and fast. Are you asking renters to call or email you? If you are, can you respond quickly? Does your online system make it simple to book and pay?

One of the things that I hear from renters time and time again is that the home they viewed online turned out to be much less than what was described. It diminished the enjoyment of their vacation and led to bad reviews for the owner. Often to alleviate this type of risk, people will book their vacation through your major competitor – a hotel chain. The assumption is that quality hotels are reputable, have no hassle check-in and check-out, with a guaranteed guest experience. Regardless of who markets your home make sure that what they say and what they show are true reflections of the property. Don't cover up issues, fix them.

Handling problems can be a significant risk area particularly if you do not live near your vacation rental. It's important for you to know in advance exactly who you can call for what type of problem. And you'll want to make sure that they will give you priority service. If they don't, and the problem is significant, you may end up refunding all or part of the rental fee to your guest.

Problem resolution is another area where a quality property management company can be a life-saver. Because they manage so many properties they have the capacity to know who the best people are at the best price for getting things done. For the same reason those service providers give them priority since they know there will be repeat business for them if they do a good job.

Bad reviews and good reviews speak for themselves. If you want your property to be rented you must have good reviews. Look at your rental process from start to finish. Ask yourself this question – how would you rate the process if you were going through it? Anything you discover that would make you unhappy will make your potential renter unhappy. Make a change.

Don't assume that just because you rented a home in a particular area before that it is legal to do so. Some people ignore local laws and HOA restrictions concerning renting their property assuming that they will never get caught. Usually this entails renting on a weekly basis when the HOA stipulates that only rentals of thirty days or more are allowed. Know the rules. Don't put yourself or your renters in jeopardy.

Vandalism

Every vacation property risks vandalism, particularly if that property is left vacant for any period of time. Online calendars, like those on most self-service sites, are targets for people looking to commit these crimes. Investing in a good security system is a must.

But beyond the vandalism created by actual criminals is the vandalism that may be caused by excessive partying or renting to individuals who just don't care about other people's property. We call this type of vandalism use/misuse/abuse. If there is one thing I find true across all destination rental properties it is that the cheaper the property is per person the higher the user damages incurred.

Having a way to "qualify" applicants before renting to them can alleviate some of the risk of user damages. Far more effective though is the ability to inspect the property prior to check-in and immediately after check-out. In this way you can determine quickly whether or not to return a security deposit. This may be difficult to do unless you've hired someone to do it on your behalf.

Wear and Tear

I'll talk about the concept of wear and tear in more detail in a later chapter but it warrants mentioning here since there are some destinations that are more susceptible to excessive wear and tear, sometimes by people and sometimes by the weather.

Beach properties are one example. Even when not intentional the furnishings in these properties are frequently stained from the oils, sunscreens or lotions used. Sand on the bottom of bare feet or sandals may ruin carpets and floors, and plug drains when washed off in the shower.

Urban residential properties tend to have the greatest risk due to weather and natural causes. These properties often rent to families whose children can be hard on a property creating a type of "natural" stress.

Mountain properties also seem to have more natural stress. This can include the great outdoors coming indoors, like animals making homes in the attic or hiking boots carrying in dirt, grime, and small gravel in warmer months, and snow, salt, and ice in the colder months. Weather extremes may be the higher risk but the wear and tear from people certainly contributes to higher maintenance.

Each destination property has its unique stresses due to property type. Care, replacement, and proper maintenance are essential to maximize income potential.

Competition

Competition from other vacation rentals in the area is a major risk factor. The more vacation rentals there are available in your area the steeper the curve in getting renters to choose yours. Competition drives rental pricing as will amenities, fresh interior design, distance to attractions and shops, services available, and privacy.

The best way to remain competitive is to update the interior of your rental at least every five years, keep the place in good condition at all times, and most importantly start by purchasing a property that offers something unique. Competitive advantage goes to the property with more sleeping capacity, uncompromised views of oceans, landscapes, cityscapes, etc. and/or less inventory of your type of unique property. For example, you may have the only three-bedroom home for rent where 90% of the properties are two-bedroom.

Rewards

Don't let all this talk about risk scare you away from owning a vacation rental. I simply wouldn't be doing my job if I didn't highlight some of the risk factors you should consider. I'm a firm believer that owning vacation rental property has more rewards than risks if you do your due diligence and treat it like the business it is.

I own several vacation rental properties. All of them are in locations that my family and

I thoroughly enjoy. This is your primary reward – you get the ability to enjoy a vacation destination that you might only have been able to afford once or twice in the past. A well-managed, well-maintained vacation rental property in a good location with a fresh interior will produce income.

With few exceptions real estate has and continues to be a viable investment strategy. As with any investment, perform due diligence and then enjoy the property you select.

PART TWO

RESPONSIBILITY OF OWNERSHIP

BUILDING YOUR BRAND

Congratulations! You've set your goals, done your due diligence, and you're now the proud owner of the perfect vacation rental property. It's time to get to work putting in place the operations that will start bringing renters and rental income to you.

As I mentioned earlier, you are competing not just with other vacation rental property owners, but also with major hotel chains and luxury resorts. Many of these are known and trusted brands.

For example, a guest checking in to a hotel or resort knows exactly what to expect based on having stayed in that brand of hotel or resort before. They are comfortable that the brand will deliver the amenities they desire. As a newly minted vacation rental property owner, you don't yet have an established brand. You need to create one. What will be the brand, reputation, and theme of your individual property?

What makes a renting guest choose you and your property over any other property in the area? Convenience and value will attract them but it's ethics and service that will keep them.

Ethics and Service

It is imperative for your success to establish an ethical reputation early and to deliver a quality product that is clean, well-maintained, fully operational, decorated to current standards, and competitive in price and features to the industry standard for your area. Accurate advertising with plenty of photographs and detailed descriptions are a must.

Ethics to me go beyond the letter of the law. I see being ethical as treating people fairly, using reasonable actions, and responding to issues in the way I would like to be treated in the same situation. It isn't always easy to separate legal behavior from ethical behavior so let me give you a few examples.

1. As an owner you are in your legal right to use your property whenever you want. But you have an ethical responsibility to schedule your private use so it does not interfere with pre-scheduled rentals. Think about how you would feel if you'd been planning a vacation for months only to find out at the last minute that the rental you had booked was no longer available.

2. Legally you have the right to decorate and stock your rental in any way you like, including using the least expensive fixtures, furniture, and amenities. Ethically though, if you are charging a top rate based on location and season, you have a responsibility to equip your rental with items that reflect the luxury price tag.

3. You may be within your rights legally to jerry-rig items to get them working, to not replace peeling paint or wallpaper, or worn carpet. But ethically you have a responsibility to maintain the property and amenities at a level that reflects the price of rental and what an average guest would expect.

4. As an owner you have the right to set standards for rental agreements, limitations on rental requirements, and restrictions for

guests in the use of your property. But you have the ethical responsibility to follow established guidelines of fair and equitable rental agreements, established and accepta-ble limitations, and fair and equitable restrictions by industry standards. The Vacation Rental Management Association (VRMA.com) is a good resource for this type of information.

On a side note, if you plan on going it alone rather than hiring a property management company, I would encourage you to join the VRMA. They offer services, materials, sup-port, and educational conferences to all members.

In terms of service, my advice is simple. Do what you say you are going to do. If you tout the fact that your reservation process is quick and easy – then make sure it is quick and easy. If you tell a renter they can call 24/7 with any problem they have – then make sure you have someone to answer the phone.

As an individual vacation rental property owner your brand is only as good as your word. Guest reviews will either make you or break you. Your reputation as a fair, honest, and ethical owner will help you maintain repeat renters and consistent rental income.

HOMEOWNERS' ASSOCIATION

A Homeowners' Association, also known as an HOA, is an organization that sets rules and regulations for a community. You would have been informed prior to closing on your vacation property whether or not it is governed by an HOA. You also should have received a copy of the Covenants, Conditions and Restrictions (CC&Rs), the Articles of Incorporation, and the Bylaws of this non-profit corporation.

HOAs exist to maintain the value of your property by imposing certain standards for all homeowners and by maintaining any common areas within the development. It is important to understand the restrictions of your HOA and state, particularly as it relates to rentals. Some HOAs impose minimum times on rentals. For example, an owner may be allowed to rent their property monthly, but not weekly. Some HOAs are friendly to allowing vacation rentals but some may charge an "impact" fee to offset what they feel may be excess damage caused by transient renters.

The HOA will likely have architectural requirements such as the colors of outside paint, the types of landscaping, whether or not satellite dishes are allowed, etc. Often there will be approval forms that must be submitted.

Then there are the regulations around uses of your property. For example, a client of mine owned a condo whose HOA restricted them from parking their vehicle in their driveway overnight. Another had strict rules about when you could set your garbage cans out and how soon after trash pick-up you had to have them back in the garage or otherwise out of sight. There may even be restrictions on the number or kind of pets you may keep.

Your guests will need to be provided with a list of these types of restrictions to ensure that they are also aware of what they can and cannot do. Otherwise you may find yourself in trouble with the HOA. You'd be amazed at how many HOAs have participating owners who like nothing better than to drive around their neighborhoods looking for violations to report.

Generally once a violation has been noted, you will receive a letter asking that it be corrected and/or that a fine has been assessed. The fines may be small depending on the infraction, but if you don't pay them, they become liens against the property which may raise questions with a future buyer should you decide to sell.

Every HOA has dues that must be paid, either monthly, quarterly or annually. They also have at least one annual meeting with many meeting monthly. There will be a Board of Directors elected yearly. Unless you have a lot of time on your hands and live close to your rental property I would recommend that you do not become involved with the inner workings of the HOA. Pay your dues, adhere to the CC&Rs, and enjoy your property.

INSURANCE

Just as for your primary residence, it is your responsibility to maintain insurance on your rental property. This includes liability insurance as well as property damage insurance. Policies for rentals are commonly called Rental Dwelling Policies, Landlord Policies, or Townhouse/Condo Dwelling Policies and can be obtained through most insurance carriers.

I recommend that you get property damage insurance in an amount equal to the replacement cost of the property. Liability insurance should be a minimum of five hundred thousand dollars ($500,000) for each occurrence. These policies should protect you in most situations. Regrettably we live in a litigious society. It just makes sense to be prepared.

Home Warranties

While we're on the subject of insurance, let's discuss home warranties. A common misconception is that these are insurance policies. They are not. They're a service contract.

You may have received a Home Warranty from the seller when you bought your home. These are usually good for one year and then the home warranty company will attempt to get you to continue your coverage. While a home warranty may give you peace of mind in your primary residence, I don't recommend them for vacation rental properties, particularly for appliances and air conditioning, and here's why:

1. They are not quick to respond to your needs. For example, let's say you have a unit whose air conditioning goes out in the middle of summer and the warranty company can't get anyone out to even look at it for three days. Well, now you've got some pretty upset renters. Same holds true if a major appliance like a stove or a washer goes out. This is becoming a huge issue on seven day rentals.

2. Home warranty companies are notoriously difficult to work with. In fact, they lead the list of most complained about companies in America in the 500 categories tracked by Angie's List.

3. You are limited to using their contractors meaning that you have to contact the warranty company first to find out who services your area, then attempt to make an appointment with them.

4. They don't always cover the entire cost of the repair or replacement. There is often a deductible and always a fee for the service call. To top it off, the replacement may not be of the same quality that was originally installed.

Needing to deal with a home warranty company to fix a problem when a renter is in your unit may seriously impede how quickly you can make that renter happy. In my opinion, you are better off saving $50 a month and putting it into a rental repair fund than you are spending that $500 or $600 per year for a home warranty.

REPAIRS AND MAINTENANCE

One thing we can count on, in addition to death and taxes, is that "things" don't last forever – they break or get worn. Ensuring your guests will happily give your property great reviews means making sure it is in tip-top shape. Repairs and maintenance are a critical responsibility of being a vacation rental property owner.

I've already discussed the challenges of working under a home warranty but what are the alternatives? Unless you live nearby and are "handy" you'll need to establish relationships with service providers – and the sooner the better. You don't want to wait until something breaks to figure out who you're going to call.

Just as you performed due diligence on the rental property before you bought it, you should perform due diligence on the major service providers that you will need. You can start by asking the neighbors around your property who they use. Or you can use recommendation sites like Angie's List or Handyman.com. Regardless of how you get the referral, it pays to visit the Better Business Bureau as well to make sure they are in good standing and have no major complaints.

Finding reliable, quality help is so difficult that it's become a major reason that vacation rental owners turn to property management companies. These firms have the local relationships and contacts to get things done quickly, correctly, and at a reasonable cost.

Some of the service providers you may want to identify upfront are:

- Housekeeping Service
- Plumber
- Painter
- General Handyman
- Air Conditioning/Heating Specialist
- Appliance Repair Specialist
- Landscaping Professional
- Pool/Spa Service
- Telephone/Internet Specialist

- Locksmith
- Pest Control Service
- Furniture Repair Specialist
- Security/Alarm Service

Wear and Tear versus Damages

Some of the items that will require repair, maintenance, or replacement may be due to wear and tear from normal use or they may be from outright damage caused by guests. Many vacation rental property owners ask for a security deposit at the time of rental to cover "damages." But often, the owner and the renter don't see eye to eye on what constitutes damages. I've provided some examples of each in the paragraphs below to give you a better feel for the difference.

Wear and tear is defined as the damage that naturally and inevitably occurs as a result of normal aging and use. It is the depreciation of an asset that is assumed to occur even when an item is used competently, with care and proper maintenance. Even the most conscientious guest will cause minor damage over the course of a rental agreement, particularly if it is long-term. Wear and tear is unavoidable and there is a certain amount that you as an owner should expect every year. Damages on the other hand are things that are out of the ordinary.

Here are some examples of the differences between wear and tear that you should expect, and damages that would be charged to the guest.

Dirty carpet in main traffic areas or small, light stains would be considered wear and tear. Burn marks, rips, pet urine, or heavy stains like red wine are damages.

Scuff marks or small nicks on walls are wear and tear. Deep gouges, holes, torn wallpaper, crayon marks, and scratches or chew marks from pets constitute damages.

Blind pulls or strings may be worn or frayed due to constant use. The internal strings that pull the blinds up and down may also become damaged from sun exposure and break – all normal wear and tear. Blinds or curtains that are torn, stained, or pulled from the frame are signs of damage.

Other things that could be construed as damages would be: a yard dug up by a pet, excessive mildew in a bathroom caused by an unreported leak, excessive dirt in other parts of the home that requires professional cleaning to remove, drains that are clogged from inserting foreign objects or items that should not be put in a drain, wood floors with deep scratches, or broken tiles on a relatively new floor that are not the result of poor installation.

Those that would be normal wear and tear would be: replacement of component parts like faucet washers, water heater elements, or pool filters. Also, if a single plate or glass is broken, or a spoon is missing, or there's a small blood stain on a towel – it is wear and tear. If several plates are broken, several pieces of silver missing, or several towels bloodstained or missing from the same renter – it would be damages.

The bottom line is that the difference between wear and tear and damages is often a judgement call. In all cases, you should strive to be fair and ethical to your guest. That being said, as an owner you should plan for and set aside money for those items that are normal wear and tear.

SAFETY AND SECURITY

It is your responsibility as a vacation rental property owner to ensure as much as possible the safety and security of your guests. Here are some tips on how to keep your guests safe and secure:

1. Ensure heavy appliances are secured. For example, if you have a large screen TV on a console it should be secured so that a small child cannot easily tip it over.

2. Pool filters should be properly covered to prevent someone's hair or clothing from being sucked in. Have access to the pool secured from young children to prevent drowning. Install non-slip texturing around the pool area if possible.

3. Each state has regulations regarding pool safety and security requirements. There may also be local regulations. Make sure

you know what they are and that you are in compliance.

4. Provide ample outdoor lighting. Use motion activated lighting if you have a single-family rental and ensure that lighting on the walkway to and from the doors is good.

5. The fire extinguisher system should be in good working order and smoke detectors should be installed to warn guests if a fire occurs.

6. Trim back bushes and trees from doors and windows on the property. This eliminates places for burglars to hide. In states like Arizona and California, it also helps to keep wildfires from spreading to the home.

7. Install durable doors with deadbolts.

8. Make sure your sliding glass doors and windows have anti-theft mechanisms. For example, use a through-the-frame pin for windows that open vertically or a dowel that fits in the track for windows that open horizontally. The dowel approach can also be used to secure a sliding glass door, or a security bar can be installed. The idea is to make a break-in less likely.

9. Consider installing a monitored alarm system even if your state or city doesn't require it.

Breakdowns in any security measures that you have in place should be considered an emergency and fixed immediately. Do everything you can to limit your liability and protect your guests, just as you would in your own home.

TAXES

First let me begin by saying I am not an accountant nor am I a tax specialist. This section is simply intended to make you aware of some of the taxes that may impact you as a result of owning a vacation rental property. I strongly urge you to consult your own accountant or tax specialist for professional assistance.

There are basically three types of taxes that may affect you and your rental property: income tax, compliance taxes, and property tax.

Income tax: Any income that you generate from the rental of your property must be reported as income tax. You may be able to deduct certain expenses related to the rental depending on how often it was occupied and how often you used the home. Check with your accountant to determine what may apply as each situation is unique.

Often it will depend on whether you are filing as an individual, an LLC, an S Corp or a Corporation.

Compliance tax: This tax may also be known as sales tax, occupancy tax, lodging tax, transient tax, room tax, or hotel tax. It is paid on the total amount of the rental fee including things like cleaning services, maintenance fees, and pet fees. Generally anything that you charge the renter is subject to the tax. These taxes are payable to the state, city or county depending on your location. They are often confusing as different rates and payment dates (monthly or quarterly) may apply.

Check with the state and city where your rental property is located to see what types of licensing you may need.

Property tax: This is the tax assessed by the state, county, and/or city where your rental property is located. If you took out a loan for the property then it's likely that your property tax is part of an escrow payment that your bank then remits on a semi-annual basis. Otherwise your property tax statement will come directly to you. It is

your responsibility to ensure that this tax is
paid.

PART THREE

SETTING GUEST EXPECTATIONS

RESPONSIBLE MARKETING

Word of mouth is great for getting rental referrals and it helps to build your brand. Unfortunately, when you're just starting out, relying on word of mouth alone can be painfully slow. To reach a larger pool of potential renters in a shorter period of time nothing is better than good old-fashioned marketing.

For the purposes of this section I am going to assume that you have decided to go it alone and are not using a vacation rental property management company. If you are using someone then skip this chapter and go right to the marketing section in Part Four – Choosing a Property Management Company.

There are many different ways to market your property including using a personal website, magazines and newspapers, travel agents, or third-party websites like VRBO and HomeAway to name a few. It is recommended that you use as many of these outlets as your budget will support to reach the greatest number of vacation renters. But regardless of where you decide to advertise the effectiveness of your marketing begins with beautiful photos and accurate descriptions.

In my company I always use a professional photographer to take pictures of a client's property. Professionals know exactly the right angle and lighting to use to show your property at its best. The more pictures you take the better and if you can add a bit of video, even better. Potential renters want to see what they are getting.

You should include all of the major rooms of the house: living, dining, kitchen, bathrooms, and bedrooms. If you have outdoor space or are in a resort or condo community with amenities outside the unit, show those as well. Keep it fresh too. Whenever you change décor, remodel, or paint – take new pictures. The guest will feel more at home right from the start if what they see when they walk in your door matches what they saw in your ads.

Descriptions are as important as photos. If you can afford to have a copywriter author your descriptions then hire one. There's an art to using the right words to describe a space in a manner that will entice renters to consider you.

For example, these two paragraphs are describing the same room in the same rental.

1. Large master bedroom with king-size bed. En-suite bathroom, balcony access.

2. Relaxation is yours in the spacious master with king-size bed. Enjoy gorgeous sunsets from your private balcony. Then lounge in the en-suite bathroom complete with multi-head shower and soaking tub.

Which paints a stronger picture? The first is just a bare-bones description while the second transports the renter into the space allowing them to visualize being there.

My only caution is that you be honest. Nothing will turn a guest off faster than being lied to. With the easy access of social media they can quickly tell the whole world you can't be trusted. So if the view of the sunset from the balcony can really only be seen if you lean over as far as you can and peek around the corner, then don't include it your description.

Third-Party Services

The emergence of third-party services for individuals to rent their properties has surged in recent years. From VRBO, to AirBnb, to HomeAway, the choices are endless and new ones seem to crop up almost daily. That's good news for you if you are willing to put in the work to go it alone.

These are fee-based services that market your property to the world – locally and internationally. They offer a wealth of information about other rental properties in your area so don't hesitate to use them to check out the competition. They also may have many of the tools you will need as a property manager. These tools include things like a member dashboard, availability calendar, rental reviews and more. There are options for annual membership to allow you to pick the level that is right for you.

As with any service, it is your responsibility to perform due diligence to ensure that what the service is offering is truly what you need. Keep in mind that you may still be responsible for responding to calls, coordinating calendars, taking payments and dealing with credit card issues. It is imperative to understand what is offered, how to best utilize the service and manage expectations from the provider.

SETTING RATES

Setting the appropriate rental rate to insure that your property has maximum occupancy is more an art than a science. It requires a thorough knowledge of the area, data on comparables and competition, and access to rental rate tools. Remember, you aren't just competing against other vacation rental owners. You're also being stacked up against resorts and hotels.

One of the key components of rate is seasonality. Unless your rental is in a year-round destination location or a place like the Florida Keys, it likely has a season. There is a particular time of the year that vacationers will flock to your destination and other times they will not.

It is important to understand that based on this seasonality, your income from the property will fluctuate as well. For example: if your property is a winter escape destination then your rates will be set higher in the months of December through March when demand is high. You'll see increased income in those months. But once the "season" has passed, in order to maintain occupancy your rates may need to be adjusted and your income in those non-season months may fall.

That's just the way the industry works. It's nothing to be concerned about, but you do need to be aware and plan for it. Of course since you did all of your due diligence before buying your property, including determining your financial goals, you should already have a good feel for what the market will bear. A word of caution – things can change rapidly. You can't set your rental rates and then assume that they will be good for years and years. A smart owner is one who stays in touch with the market and adjusts his/her rates as needed.

Speaking of planning, if the primary goal for owning your vacation rental is income generation, try to schedule your personal enjoyment of the property to avoid "high" season. If you don't, you may be missing out on what could be some significant income.

TAKING RESERVATIONS

Attractive rates, awesome location, and effective marketing will bring potential renters to your door. But if you can't welcome them in, you've lost them. Having a reservation system that is real-time and easy to use is a must.

First – do not underestimate the time you will spend on bookings. There will always be questions a renter wants answered that are not readily apparent. For example, a friend of mine was booking a vacation for her family which included a two year-old. She couldn't tell from the photos or the description of the condo whether or not a Pack-n-Play would fit it the bedroom. The unit also included a pool so she needed to know if life-jackets were provided or she needed to bring her own for the little guy. She had to call.

No matter how thorough you think you've been in describing the property, renters will need to know more. You'll need to respond rapidly, at a minimum within 24 hours, if you want a shot at booking them. Email is great but you should also plan for spending time on the phone.

The amount of time it takes to answer questions and deal with renters during the reservation process is a primary reason why many owners make the decision to use a vacation rental property management firm like mine. We have the staff and resources available 24/7 to work with renters at times that are convenient for them.

For those of you do-it-yourselfers who want an automated software system here are some things I recommend getting. It should include a user-friendly booking module, excellent channel management, and easy to use templates for setting up an enticing website.

Once you purchase one of these systems it is up to you to learn how to use it. Although helpdesk support is available, you are still pretty much on your own to make it work. Another option if you like the ability to be independent but don't want to totally go it alone is to consider a franchise. The value and growth potential coupled with the support and back-end systems make this an affordable option, even for beginners. My company utilizes proprietary, state-of-the-art technology and operational processes. We have a franchise program available and I would be happy to discuss it with you.

LEGAL ISSUES

As I mentioned at the beginning of this book, once you make a decision to rent your vacation property you have made a decision to enter into a business. Businesses come with their own set of rules and regulations. Here are a few that you should consider. Keep in mind that I am not a lawyer and I am not giving you legal advice. The issues listed below are for your consideration. You should discuss them with the appropriate professionals.

Business Type

One of the first decisions you will want to make is to determine your business type. Will you be an individual, a sole proprietor, a LLC, or some other type of corporation? Each of these business types will have its own set of rules for reporting rental income. They will also determine the name that you use for licensing and registration. If you do decide to incorporate in some form, you may want to do so in the state where your property is located. In some cases it may make the licensing and registration process easier.

Licensing

In most locations, renting a property on a short-term basis is considered a business which requires obtaining a business license or licenses, sometimes referred to as a registration. Your assigned license number is then used in the collecting, reporting and remitting of sales, lodging, and occupancy taxes from your guests. The definition of short-term varies by state. It is usually less than 30 days but can be as long as 6 months in states like Florida and Hawaii.

While choosing a business type is optional (you can remain an individual) registering and getting licensed is not. Often there are requirements for city, county, and state licensing so it's important to understand the requirements for each level of govern-ment agency. You can accomplish this by visiting the websites of the agencies where your property is located or contacting them by phone. Be sure to inquire about the reporting requirements for your rental activity as well. Depending on the amounts you may not have to file monthly. A good property management company will handle updating and maintaining all of this for you.

Rental Agreements

A well-written rental agreement protects both you and the renter, defining the legal relationship between you and your guests. In essence it lays out exactly how you wish your home to be treated and describes your expectations to the renter.

I strongly recommend that you use a rental agreement with each renter. There are several boilerplate forms available online for free that you can obtain and customize for your needs. At a minimum your rental agreement should spell out:

- Names of all of the parties to the agreement
- Check-in and check-out dates
- Rental rate and payment schedule including any security deposit

- Cancellation policy
- Refund policy including how and when the security deposit will be refunded
- House rules and policies regarding such things as cleaning fees, pets, smoking, pool use, noise, etc.

Agreements with Third-Parties

While not required, you may also wish to have agreements drawn up with your third-party service providers. These would be services that you use on a regular basis such as housecleaners, landscapers, or house-sitters who check on your property when it is not occupied. These agreements would define things like normal scheduling, fees, emergency response time, communication requirements, etc.

HOA Requirements

Many HOAs that allow for short-term rentals have reporting requirements of their own. Often it is the property owner's responsibility to let the HOA know when the property is rented, for how long, and by whom. Sometimes they require even more detail such as the make, model, and license plate number of any vehicles belonging to the renters. You'll want to make sure that you understand these requirements and submit the appropriate information to avoid fines and to keep your guests from being questioned or hassled.

AMENITIES

When a potential guest is researching a rental property for their vacation they are generally looking at four things: location, internal amenities, external amenities, and price. I talked earlier about pricing and how it is affected by location and seasonality. Since you've already purchased your vacation rental, those two criteria have been pre-determined. What hasn't is what you put in and around your home. This also has a major impact on the price you can charge and fortunately, it is one you can control.

Earlier, in the chapter on choosing a location, we spoke about external amenities, those things that surround your home or are in close proximity to it. Equally important, but often overlooked are the amenities inside your home. These include not only the layout and design of your home, i.e. number of bedrooms, number of bathrooms, living room, den, etc. but also the home's furnishings and inventory. Let's take a look at each of these in more detail.

Internal Amenities

By far the most important internal amenity is the one listed above – number of bedrooms. But it isn't just the number that is important. It's also the size and comfort of the bed, easy access to a bathroom, and suitable closet space.

En-suite bathrooms are the most desirable and can garner a higher rental value, especially if they are equipped with Jacuzzi tubs, multi-head shower systems, dual sinks, or heated floors. And don't forget the lighting – ample lighting in the bathroom is a must for make-up application. The lack of lighting can give a bad start to a guest's day.

Other examples of internal amenities would be a separate laundry room, workout room, three-car garage, or an in-home theater.

Cable or satellite TV, and wireless internet access are no longer "nice to haves." In today's online world, your property must come with these in order to compete. Internet speed should be fast. No one wants to wait 30 seconds or more for a website to load. I also recommend your television service provide at least one premium channel.

Furnishings

Furnishings are things like appliances, couches, chairs, tables, beds, and permanent fixtures such as built-ins and lighting in the home. You are listing your property as a "luxury" vacation rental and as such, a guest will have expectations regarding the quality of the furnishings they will find upon arrival. Studies have shown that the first nine minutes of a stay will lock in 80% of a guest's opinion of their entire experience in your rental.

In all cases you should strive for the highest quality you can afford but you also need to insure its durability. While a gray satin couch might look stunning in the family room, it stains easily and is difficult to clean. The same could be said for a white shag rug. It may look trendy and rich but in a high traffic area its deep piles will collect dirt and without frequent cleaning it may soon become an eyesore.

Another thing to keep in mind when choosing furnishings for your vacation rental is decorating trends. The interior design industry estimates that homeowners redecorate every five years to keep their homes looking fresh. This can get quite expensive when you're talking about changing out couches or carpet. But your guests are expecting a fresh and modern vacation rental, not one that is dated.

So what do you do? Start with neutrals in all your major pieces. For kitchen appliances that means going with stainless steel. Stainless steel has been a mainstay in kitchens for the last century and no one predicts its obsolescence anytime soon. It adds a polished finish to any décor and seamlessly matches with all color schemes.

Couches, love seats, tables and chairs should match the "vibe" of wherever your vacation rental is located. So for example, if your property is located near the beach, you may have wicker furniture. If you are in the mountains, a more rustic wood finish would be appropriate, and in the desert you might go with a southwest flare. What you don't want to do is put ultra-modern, minimalist, sterile pieces in a cozy, mountain chalet or wicker-based furniture in a New York City high-rise.

Regardless of location you'll want your fabrics in neutral colors like gray, tan, taupe, black, or sand. I would warn against pure white unless it is in a highly wearable, easy to clean fabric. When choosing fabric also keep in mind how it will be used. If your rental is a beach property you should expect that oils and lotions will get on the furniture. You'll need a fabric that repels oils or at least cleans well.

Location will determine what other special amenities you might need to have. For example, if you have a ski chalet you'll need to make sure that there is a place for renters to leave their boots and snow-covered clothes where they won't harm your floors or furniture. In a beach location you'll want to stay away from rugs that will collect sand no matter how often you vacuum.

I also recommend when you are thinking about window treatments you choose those that are uncomplicated and least likely to break. For that reason I like to see rod and ring type curtains rather than string pull curtains or shades. Everyone knows how to open them, the rings rarely break and the curtains are easy to take down, clean and replace.

Window treatments should also block a great deal of light when pulled. A common complaint that we receive from guests is that the shades, blinds or curtains do not block enough of the sunlight. I recently stayed at a hotel in San Jose Del Cabo and I really appreciated that the window had enough blocking ability to keep the room dark during the day. It was an east facing room and I had travelled all night to get there. Having a dark room made it easier for me to rejuvenate.

The style of your bedroom furniture should also match the motif of your location. A king size bed is a must in the master bedroom if space permits. We've had renters pass on the ideal place simply because the master bedroom had a queen instead of a king. Guest bedrooms may contain queen size beds or two twin beds.

When deciding what to do with your guest room, take into account your target market for renters. If you're going after male golfers or families with older children, then twin beds might make sense. If the majority of your renters will be couples or parents with younger children then queens or kings are the way to go. You may also want to scope out the competition before deciding. If everyone has queens in the second bedroom then you may want to set yourself apart by having twins.

Mattresses should be medium-firm and, unless the bed is a platform model, they should be set on a box-spring. Memory foam is also great for accommodating the majority of sleepers' needs. Cushion top mattress pads are recommended for added comfort. Just make sure that you get ones that won't trap heat. Renters will pull them off if they make the bed uncomfortable.

Another item that should be in each bed-room is a newer model television. Reading lamps on each side of the bed are also necessary.

Once you have the basic furnishings it is easy to keep your property looking fresh. A new coat of paint in a trending color, plus accent pieces like throw pillows, vases, and wall art that can be swapped out at minimal expense are all it takes.

You may want to consider utilizing the expertise of an interior designer when determining how to decorate and furnish your rental. A designer often has a better feel for what works in the area, can steer you in the right direction in terms of color usage, and has access to deals with suppliers that could save you a significant amount of money. A beautifully decorated property that meets guest expectations helps to keep them coming back again and again.

Inventory

Inventory may be thought of as all the wear and tear types of items you typically would find in a home. This would include kitchen and bathroom linens, small appliances like coffee makers and vacuums, pots and pans, dinnerware, silverware, garbage cans, irons and ironing boards, etc. A full list of the items that might be in your rental can be found in Appendix A.

As with furnishings, you should equip your property with the highest quality of items that you can afford. However, if you are outside the United States you may need to get your items from local sources.

Nowhere is quality more of an issue than in the bedroom. Many people consider the bedroom their oasis. Bedding must be inviting, stylish, and scream luxury. If the current bedding trend is to have multiple decorative pillows, then you need to have multiple decorative pillows. Coverlets may look great alone but if you really want to impress you need a coverlet and a high-end comforter.

Sheets should be luxurious as well. A thread count of 400 or more is recommended. Get washable duvets to cover your blankets. Avoid microfiber. Though white sheets may not last as long as colored sheets, they still are the number one look, symbolizing elegant simplicity.

White is the color that guests used to staying in high-end hotels have come to expect. Hotels spend fortunes funding studies to understand guest psychology. The results show a primal association between the color white and cleanliness. If you see crisp white sheets you instantly know they are clean. Sheets that are some other color like gray or maroon might be clean but who knows? Those colors hide dirt and guests subconsciously know this.

Bright freshly laundered sheets look clean and therefore appear more sanitary.

White sheets are actually easier to clean and maintain. They can be bleached and washed in hot water which keeps them whiter, longer. Plus they always match. White is white. You don't have to buy a full set if all you need to replace are some pillow cases.

Bath towels should be plush and hold up well when washed. No one likes to dry themselves off with something that feels like sandpaper. Believe me I've been in many a luxury hotel where the towels felt just like that. It wasn't a pleasant experience and made me wonder why I was paying top dollar to stay there.

It's also important to have matching white linens and towels throughout the home. It gives your home a "put together" feel. It also makes it easier for the cleaning service to ready your home again once the laundry has been done since there is no decision about which towels or sheets go where.

Quality may be less distinguishable in the balance of the other items of inventory in your home. For example, there isn't a noticeable difference in performance between a silverware set that costs $70 and one that costs $150, or a kitchen towel that costs $6 versus one that costs $9. Given the fact that these items need to be replaced frequently, it may even be advisable to go the less expensive route.

What is important to consider for silverware, dinnerware, or pots and pans is how easy it will be to match the current set with replacement pieces in the future. Simple white plates with rounded shapes are much easier to replace than a seasonal design. I recommend taking a picture of the box that your items came in so you always know the style and the manufacturer.

When buying look for items that say "open stock." These are the easiest to replace. You started with matching sets of flatware, dishes, pots, pans and storage containers and you want to maintain that appearance. Your kitchen drawers and cabinets should never look like everything came from a garage sale.

Closets, drawers, and cabinets regardless of where they are in your home should be free of any of your personal effects. Find an area in your home, perhaps a laundry room closet or storage area in the garage, that can be locked and store your personal items there. That way they are secure and not accessible to renters or service providers.

The bottom line is to put yourself in the shoes of the guest who is renting your property. What quality would you expect for the price you are asking your guests to pay? If you must budget, do it somewhere other than the bedrooms or bathrooms.

INSPECTIONS

In the earlier chapter on repairs and maintenance I spoke about the differences between damages and normal wear and tear. Damages may reduce the amount returned to a renter from their security deposit. Wear and tear does not. Problems arise when the owner and the renter do not see eye to eye about the issue.

To avoid any misunderstandings it is helpful to have performed an inspection both before the guest arrives and immediately after they leave. Ideally you should take photos during each inspection. A photo provides visual proof of the condition of your rental property prior to a guest's use and after. It will alleviate a renter's ability to say, "It was that way we when we got here."

If you don't live close to your vacation rental property this becomes much more difficult to do. It's another reason that many owners prefer to work with a vacation rental property management company. However, it may be possible to set up an arrangement with your cleaning service to provide these inspections. Don't be surprised however if they won't take any liability of damages for missing or unseen items. You'll need to spell out exactly what you are looking for in your contract with them and be prepared to pay an extra fee for this service.

Let your renters know up front that you do inspections and include the information in your rental agreement. Renters may be more considerate of how they treat your property if they know that someone will be checking.

GUEST FEEDBACK

I'm a firm believer that every guest should be invited to leave feedback on their stay. I encourage feedback because it helps me to ensure that I am providing the best possible guest experience. It lets me know what they really enjoyed and what needs to be improved. Sometimes guest feedback is the only way to know when minor things aren't working – things your maintenance or cleaning service wouldn't ordinarily catch.

Take for instance an iron that doesn't get hot or has stopped producing steam. Or maybe it's a toaster that burns the bread no matter what setting you turn it to. These are issues you only discover by living in the place and using it. They often aren't major enough to generate a call from the renter during their stay but certainly something the renter would be happy to report in a survey.

ost hotels and resorts routinely send guest experience surveys to their customers after a stay and you should too. It's best to nip problems in the bud before they become major issues.

Pay attention also to the customer reviews that are placed either on your website, on third-party websites, or any other social media site. Set up Google Alerts so anytime the name of your rental or your name is mentioned online you get notified. Take these reviews seriously. An independent review by a guest carries considerable value and can directly impact your ability to gain future renters.

Take action where appropriate on any suggestions that a guest may leave. If they've had a valid negative experience, respond to them. People simply want to be valued and know they've been heard. A sincere apology for their trouble and a thank you for their suggestions may even incentivize them to remove the damaging review.

TO PET OR NOT TO PET

That is indeed the question and it comes up frequently. I usually advise against allowing pets in your rental. However, times they are a changin' as Bob Dylan would say.

The American Pet Products Association estimates that Americans own 83 million dogs and 95 million cats. That means that between 45 and 50% of "homeowners" has at least one dog or one cat. That's a pretty large segment of the population. And pet owners love their pets – sometimes I think more than they love their own children!

Pet owners tend to have higher incomes. They are more likely to want to vacation with their pets, particularly if they are going to be gone for an extended period of time. More and more high-end, boutique hotels are becoming pet friendly for this very reason.

Even given this trend I still lean toward no pets. However, here are some of the pros and cons to pet or not to pet so that you can make an informed decision.

Pros:

1. A larger pool of potential guests to draw from. In addition those guests tend to rent for longer periods of time.

2. Your property may become more desirable because there aren't as many options to choose from.

3. You can charge a higher rent and increase your revenue stream.

4. A guest who really can't be without their dog or cat may bring them anyway – even though you have specifically said that pets are not allowed.

Cons:

1. Potential for damage to the property. You should consider the cost to replace or repair the furnishings and surroundings of your rental. Large dogs' nails can mar hardwood floors. All dogs, particularly females, can turn the grass brown from urination. And if any pet, dog or cat, urinates in the house

itself carpet may need to be replaced. Dogs may gnaw on cabinets or door jambs and cats may scratch those and furniture as well. Will the potential cost of replacement or the lack of usability while repairs are being made outweigh the increased rental?

2. Physical injury to neighbors or other guests that your renter invites into the home. A dog bite or cat scratch can be quite serious.

3. Pets may cause a noise nuisance particularly if the guest is off doing fun things for the majority of the day and the pet is left alone. Both cats and dogs have been known to meow or bark until their owners return.

4. Allergens and dander will find their way deep into your carpets and into the air ducts. Even with a very thorough cleaning it is difficult to eliminate these entirely, which may cause problems for future guests who have pet allergies.

While the following are not pros or cons they are things you should take into consideration as well when making your decision.

1. What type of rental unit do you have? Check with your Condo Association or HOA

to determine their restrictions on pets. Also, keep in mind that a condo with walls that are shared by connected neighbors may be prone to noise complaints. The irony is that most Condo Associations have a limit on the weight of the pet, usually 50 lbs. or less. These small pets are often the most yappy and excitable.

2. Does your insurance policy cover damage from pets that are not yours? And even more important, does your liability coverage protect you from paying for physical injury caused to another by a guest's pet?

3. If you do decide that the benefits of allowing pets outweigh the risks, consider having your attorney draft a pet agreement as an addendum to the standard rental agreement that everyone signs regardless of whether or not they are bringing a pet. In the agreement you might include things such as: how many pets are allowed (limit to 2), the size of the pets (50lbs or less), who pays for additional cleaning or damage if needed, requiring papers showing that pets have been spayed or neutered and vaccinated.

4. Check the Americans with Disabilities Act (ADA) and Fair Housing Association (FHA) rules, both State and Federal, for the area in which your rental property resides. If a guest or you as a rental property owner fall under these parameters the guest may be allowed to bring a Service, Guide, Signal, or Support animal with them regardless of whether or not you typically allow pets. One exception is if allowing the pet would cause "undue hardship" on the property owner. An example of undue hardship would be if you had a severe allergic reaction to pet dander. In that case you may be able refuse to accept pets under the ADA.

BOATS, TRUCKS, AND VACATION RENTALS

You're probably wondering why, in a book about owning a vacation rental, I've decided to talk about boats and trucks. Well it's quite simple really – they're all things your friends and family like to use.

Ever notice when you get a new boat everyone is suddenly interested in going to the lake? Or when you get a new truck how family, friends, or even friends of friends suddenly have all kinds of things they need moved or picked up? And hey, they'd be happy to pay for gas, or get you a pizza and a six pack. You've instantly become the most popular person in town.

The same will be true as soon as word gets out that you now own a vacation rental. And the sweeter the location the more bees you will attract. Now I'm not saying that you shouldn't ever share the bounty with your family and friends, but I would caution you to be smart about it.

You originally decided to rent your vacation home because: a) you want to offset the cost of your mortgage and upkeep and/or b) you want to make additional income. Renting to family and friends rarely does either of those, particularly if you are renting to them during "the season" when you could have been bringing in top dollar. I recommended that you not use your property during season, and I strongly encourage you not to rent at a discount during this time to friends and family as well.

I know it's hard to say no, especially to family. That's another reason why owners elect to use a rental property management company. A company like mine can let you off the hook so you don't have to be the bad guy. You simply let them know that you've contracted with a management company that they need to call regarding booking and payment. Problem solved.

"A vacation spot out of season always has a very special magic." Max von Sydow, actor

PART FOUR

PROPERTY MANAGEMENT COMPANIES

CHOOSING

Oh if making money from your vacation home was as simple as just putting a listing up on a website and waiting for the reservations to start rolling in. Unfortunately, it's not. You have to know what you're doing. If you go it alone it could easily take years before you figure out the best websites, partners, ads and operational processes you need. How well, or how poorly, a property is managed directly impacts how profitable it will be. To make the most of your investment it's often a wise choice to hire an expert. But how do you know when you've got the right one?

There's often a bit of anxiety that goes with choosing a property manager whether it's your first vacation rental or you're leaving one management company and hiring a new one. And, since your vacation property typically isn't close to you, it's critical that you choose a manager you can trust. You want to know that your investment and your guests are in good hands.

Lots of companies and individuals tout themselves as property managers these days. To ensure that you contract with a qualified company that can meet your expectations and goals, consider asking these ten crucial questions:

1. Are they licensed for vacation rental property management?

All legally operating property management companies must have a Licensed Real Estate *Brokerage*. A Real Estate license alone is not enough; it must be a Broker's license. All brokerages are subject to the standards and statutes of the State's Department of Real Estate Commissioner.

If a property manager is collecting, holding, and negotiating reservations for you they must have a legally operating trust account. For your benefit as an owner this means they are held to a higher standard in terms of securing your money in a trust account and keeping records in a specific manner.

Also, depending on the market, your properties can be listed on local MLS for better exposure and rental opportunities.

2. What does their management fee cover?

All property management companies are not created equal. Don't assume that since one company offers a concierge service for guests that all companies do. Many say they offer a concierge service but it's really just a number to a third-party company. Get a detailed list of exactly what services are covered in the fee. Are all the services you require offered? Remember you're hiring a property management company because you don't have the time or expertise to do it yourself. Don't let what you thought was a great deal end up costing you in time or money.

3. How will my home be marketed?

Let's face it – an empty rental home generates no income. To ensure your home is rented as often as you'd like means reaching as many potential vacationers as possible. You can't do that effectively if the only advertising your property management company is doing is through their own website, word of mouth referrals, and the MLS listings. But it isn't just where the company advertises but how they advertise. Do they know the difference between an ad that sells and one that doesn't? Do they know how to recognize a qualified inquiry from a looky-loo? Do they follow up on inquiries within 24 hours?

4. How easy is it for me or my renters to contact you?

It's a fact of life that most real estate agents are not manning the phone all day and all night. They are busy selling homes and trying to acquire new listings for sale. While some individuals today are comfortable making their reservations online, the majority of your renters want to speak to a real person. Answering the phone or responding to an email quickly builds credibility and increases a renter's confidence by letting them know they are working with someone who will be attentive to their needs both before and during their stay. Losing a reservation because a potential renter can't reach a live person is not the kind of service you should expect.

5. What is your guest screening and check-in process?

A vacation rental home is a significant investment – one that isn't made lightly. This last thing you need is to have someone come in and trash the place; particularly if the person you thought you had rented to turned out not to be the person who showed up for the keys. There are also implications of the Fair Housing and Landlord Tenant Acts. Make sure that the property management company you choose has a screening process in place that doesn't discriminate.

6. Do you check on my home, both inside and out, when the property isn't rented?

There are several reasons why you need someone to check on your home when it isn't in use. One is to ensure that there aren't any minor issues that could turn into major problems, i.e. water leaking, toilets that don't flush, or an air conditioning system that isn't working properly. Another is to ensure that landscaping and pool services are being performed as scheduled.

7. What happens when you find there are damages?

The longer you own a vacation rental the higher the likelihood that at some point you will experience damage. It doesn't really matter if the damage was caused accidentally or on purpose, the important thing is how quickly will it be discovered and repaired. A quality company will do inspections before and after a guest's stay similar to those I suggested for you. They should also have a cadre of professional partners, ready to call, that have been vetted for providing excellent service at a reasonable price.

You should also ask about their approval process for making repairs. Does the management company call you for everything or is there a dollar amount over which they call? How do they handle emergency situations when you can't be reached?

Also inquire as to how and when they refund security deposits. Some management companies, like mine, may also have guests purchase a mandatory damage waiver which protects against damages.

8. How do you handle maintenance?

Keeping your property in pristine condition is critical to impressing guests, generating return visitors, and garnering great reviews. You want to know that the company you choose is committed to maintaining your property the way you would.

Ask about what constitutes routine maintenance such as changing light bulbs and filters versus major maintenance such as siding that needs to be replaced or the exterior needs painting. Find out how they communicate maintenance issues and its performance, particularly if it is major. Are you getting photos of the damage before and after it is repaired? Ask if they have a "No Surprises" guarantee on their statements meaning that you'll never see a charge that you didn't know about in advance.

9. Do they collect and remit the appropriate city, county and state taxes?

Taxes can be complicated when it comes to vacation rentals. Federal, state, and local municipalities all have taxes that are required when you rent your property as a vacation rental. Not only can the sales tax, transient tax, and sometimes HOA fees be calculated differently depending on your location, but also the length of stay, or in some cases how often you rented the unit during the year may have an impact.

You'll want to make sure that the company you select has experts in collecting and remitting the taxes in your location. Be sure that there are clear methods of reporting matters so that you have peace of mind knowing your liability is being handled correctly.

10. Do they have CPA oversight of their trust account?

In many states there is no requirement to have the trust account for your monies audited by a CPA. But maybe there should be. In recent years, states have started cracking down on unscrupulous property managers. Unfortunately, this is often too late for the owners when it's discovered that the money that should have been in the trust has been used to finance the property manager's lifestyle.

CASAGO

In the pages of this book I have done my best to give you the primary information you need to know and consider when becoming a vacation rental property owner. By now you have a good understanding of what it takes to manage a property on your own and what questions to ask should you decide to hire a professional. I trust you've found it helpful.

At this point I'd like to tell you a little bit about my company, Casago, and why I believe we are one of the top vacation rental property managers in the country. I do this as a frame of reference for you when speaking with other companies.

At Casago our number one priority is to meet the needs of our homeowners – to exceed every expectation. Casago is your advocate; acting as your proxy in dealings with guests, service providers, and taxing entities. We treat and manage your property as if it were our own. After all, we're owners ourselves and can easily relate to your questions and concerns. We want to make sure that your vacation rental experience is positive so that you can enjoy all the benefits that come with ownership without having to worry about all the little day-to-day details.

We are a Licensed Real Estate Broker with over 20 years' experience in vacation rental property management. Our brokers and agents have thorough knowledge of the current laws such as the Landlord Tenant Act and the National Fair Housing law to ensure Casago is operating your property in a legal manner.

There is a saying that people do business with people they know, like and trust. Trust means building rapport, listening, anticipating your needs, proactively volunteering information, avoiding problems in advance, and efficient, effective service recovery if problems occur. My success in this business is due in large part to my trustworthiness and adherence to a code of ethics. These are values that I, and the rest of my team, hold dear.

Ethics

Merriam-Webster Dictionary defines ethics as: *rules of behavior based on ideas of what is morally good or bad.*

You'll notice that the definition says "morally" but not "legally." There's a big difference here – at least to my way of thinking. For example: if we represent a property that is located next to a railroad track we would disclose that to a prospective guest. Legally we are not required to do so, but morally it's the right thing to do.

There are many property managers out there who readily take advantage of both owners and renters. They are the ones who give the industry a bad name. I want to change that.

We are committed to treating you, and your renters, honestly and fairly. It starts with the marketing of your property and goes all the way to payment of revenues. We communicate frequently so that you always know what is happening with your home. We always share our survey results with you from renters, regardless if they are good or bad.

Communication is key – it's what builds relationships and trust. We encourage the dialogue to flow both ways. You can call us any time you have a question or concern. We're here to help.

Marketing

With over 20 plus years in the business we've written thousands of ads. We know exactly what to say and where to say it to generate a high number of *qualified* applicants for your property. Our brokers and agents are sales people who have the talent to close, whether discussing with a prospect by phone, via email, or taking them on a showing.

When it comes to advertising we have you covered. Marketing locally, nationally, and internationally, we employ a multi-channel strategy to maximize occupancy. We market your property through our own website which receives 7.5 million hits per month. In addition we advertise in online market-places such as HomeAway, VRBO, FlipKey, AirBnB, and others. We provide seamless synchronization with their calendars for maximum exposure and lead management.

Our software is also designed to integrate with GDS (Global Distribution Systems) and wholesalers such as Booking.com, Expedia.com and Hotels.com. I personally visit Austin, Texas each year to meet with the leaders of VRBO and HomeAway.com to ensure we receive maximum exposure and discounts for our property owners and guests. This would be impossible for the average vacation rental owner to do on their own.

INSTEAD OF 5 MILLION VISITORS PER MONTH, WITH ONLY HOMEAWAY, VRBO, BOOKING.COM, EXPEDIA, AND AIRBNB YOU ARE GETTING MUCH MORE:

OUR OTHER SITES, 8 MILLION PER MONTH COMBINED
ADDED TOGETHER YOU WILL HAVE ABOUT 262.5 MILLION VISITORS PER MONTH.

We only use professional photos and videos when marketing your home. A professional photographer knows exactly what angles, lighting, and features to use to capture your vacation rental at its best. Great looking photos set your home apart from all the others.

Our experienced copywriters will detail the unique features of your home in an honest and engaging manner.

Setting Rates

As you know, seasonal rates have a season. But determining exactly what that season is and how you should be priced for it takes a lot of market knowledge and a strategic pricing strategy. Our company has been in this arena long enough to have developed these strategies so that you, the owner, benefits.

What we have done is create a pricing strategy that gets you booked first when it's slow in order to keep occupancy going. However, during high season, the strategy is designed to let the low-ballers get off the market first so you can rent at the highest rate for your type of property.

We use our practical knowledge of comps in the area for single and family houses, condos, townhouses, and resorts to determine a monthly base rate for both high and low seasons. We use that baseline to come up with our weekly and daily rates.

For example, take a home with a monthly rental rate of $8,000. We would take the monthly price divided by four and then add 50% to arrive at the weekly rate. ($8,000/4) x 1.5 = $3,000

Once we have the weekly rate, we break it down farther to arrive at the daily rate. Using the weekly rate of $3,000 we would divide it by 7 and then add 40% rounding up to get an even number. ($3,000/7) x 1.4 = $586

If we know that weekends are busier rental times than weekdays, we may adjust the weekend rate higher and the weekday rate lower. This is where our expert knowledge of the market is a benefit to you. You can be assured that you are getting the best rental rates.

The example above is for illustration purposes. Market forces and demand are fluid and constantly changing. Devising the right pricing strategy is often more an art than a science. Remaining flexible and alert is key.

We are constantly monitoring and assessing market, demand, and economic changes in the areas where our vacation rental owners have property. This allows us to react quickly and adjust our rate strategy accordingly in order to benefit our owners.

Operations

In my opinion, one of the greatest benefits of using a property management company is having an advocate representing your best interests handling the business in your absence. All the nitty-gritty details are taken care of – you just sit back, make major decisions, and enjoy your added income. The management fee to us covers all these details, as well as the marketing and advertising I mentioned above.

First and foremost in the nitty-gritty category, and often the most stressful for an owner, is dealing with renters. Finding them and keeping them; the good ones that is. This is where our years of experience really shine. We know the warning signs to look for in prospective renters. Think of us as the moat and drawbridge around your property. We know how to get you high quality tenants and avoid rental scams.

Our screening process begins with a consistent, standard application. Every renter gets a public record, credit, background, and criminal record check; each of which are reviewed by experienced agents who can quickly spot red flags.

Once the ideal renter applies, our 24/7 reservation process makes it easy for them to schedule their stay. Whether they call the office or they go online, there is always someone available to help them get booked. When a change needs to be made, we take care of cancellations and re-bookings. Our average response time to rental inquires is 47 minutes during regular business hours. We handle all payments and deposits.

In addition we do personalized check-ins for all of our guests at our welcome center. Here guests receive their welcome package containing keys and directions to the rental property. We use this visit to make a copy of the guest's driver's license. By confirming the renter's identity we can verify that the person checking into your home is the same person who made the reservation.

While it may be a bit inconvenient for the guest, we feel it's much safer for our owners than using a lockbox. Not only have we met the renters, but we aren't advertising an unoccupied home by having a lockbox on the door.

Every owner and guest is surveyed electronically upon check-out. All surveys are measured to find trends, problems, and points of excellence in both service and facilities. Owners are notified through the software system when there are issues with their property. We then work with you, or on our own, to provide solutions. Our custom-built survey allows us to select which comments will be posted to social media and on our website reviews.

All of our maids and maintenance staff are given iPads loaded with our exclusive software. This enables our team to communicate issues, cleaning status, and take photos of damage and repairs. They can also create work orders in the field and coordinate efficiently with each other. These property management apps are just one example of an "industry first" that did not exist before they were created by our company.

Part of this cutting-edge, online technology is the owner portal where you can check the status of your property at any time. You have access to an exclusive smartphone app that integrates directly with our software. This app allows you to see your reservation calendar and even make your own reservation. You are also able to create work orders for your property with photos of what you want fixed and update your inventory items by submitting photos of the items, receipts for new items, or removing existing items from the list.

As you can see, one of the things that make us unique from other property managers is the amount of communication we have with our owners. Our software is customizable so that you may set the level of involvement and notification that is right for you. Regardless, the system is available to you 24/7 whenever you want to view your records.

But we don't just "push" information to you. We are also firmly committed to responding when you contact us. Our belief is that all emails should be answered within 24 hours. We monitor and measure our adherence to this standard on a weekly basis and take steps quickly to rectify any issues that keep us from meeting it.

Property Maintenance

Your property is inspected prior to and immediately following a guest's stay. Keeping your property in excellent condition is vital to our reputation in the industry. That is why we do a pre-arrival inspection and a check-out inspection by our maintenance team, cleaning and inspection by our maids, and then a final inspection by the supervisor of the maids. Nobody has more eyes on your property before and after a stay than we do. Keeping your rental home in good working order is critical to keeping your unit rented with repeat guests. We are a property management company that is actively involved in making sure your investment stays in tip-top shape.

When it comes to repairs, major or minor, we have in-house maintenance staff and/or a network of licensed, bonded and insured contractors. These are providers with whom we have built relationships and know that they provide quality service at a reasonable price. Your renters also have access to 24/7 on-call emergency maintenance so you never have to worry that you'll get a call in the middle of the night. All work is documented with photos before and after so there is never a question of what was done or why.

Safety, security, and protection of your property are primary concerns. Therefore our basic maintenance also extends to monthly visits and inspections if, for any reason your property is not occupied for a period of time. Our goal is to catch minor issues before they become major problems.

Every year we do a 25 point inspection that includes things such as filter replacement, light bulbs, batteries for remote controls and smoke detectors, walking the property inside and out, and reporting on any issues that we find. We have integrated a special GPS system in our cars, maintained by an independent third party, who automatically notifies you whenever any of our vehicles come to your home. In many markets we also provide electronic locks that record the time and date of any entry into the home. These locks are state-of-the-art and provide an audit trail that cannot be changed by anyone in our office. You never have to take our word for it – you'll instantly know when we've visited your property allowing you peace of mind.

We also have a No Surprise Statement Guarantee. If we can't prove that we sent the information and photos before the work was done . . . IT'S FREE!! Our transparency, amazing staff, and custom built technology make our program the best in the industry.

Tax Collection

Casago will calculate, collect, and pay all add-on taxes on your behalf. We ensure that when we take reservations for your property that we are doing it legally, ethically, and morally. Some companies may not collect these taxes, while others may pass on what they've collected back to you to make the tax payments yourself. We make it easy by doing all the work and giving you the type of reporting you need to feel comfortable.

CPA Oversite

This is something we feel strongly about and you should too. We have hired a CPA,

in addition to our regular full-time accountant, to perform a monthly audit of our
books. We have taken the extra steps to
ensure that your trust funds are handled
appropriately. This is a rarity in the vacation rental industry. Sure, it costs us more
to do this but we want our owners to know
we understand and respect that we have a
fiduciary responsibility when it comes to
their money.

IN CONCLUSION

Vacation rental properties offer exceptional opportunities for years of enjoyment and investment income for owners. If you set realistic goals and do your due diligence you can be successful. Just don't spend so much time on the strategic plan that you never move on to purchasing and enjoying.

I've given you the tools and information that you'll need if you decide to handle the management of the property and rental process on your own. But after years and years of seeing inexperienced vacation rental property owners fail, I'd be remiss if I didn't recommend that when you are just starting out it pays to hire a professional.

So I'd like to invite you to explore a partnership with my organization whether as a franchise owner or a standalone client. Our system is proven, our staff is professional, and our support is unmatched in the industry.

For more information please contact our corporate offices at:

Casago
7655 E Redfield Rd., Suite 3
Scottsdale, AZ 85260

Phone: 480-429-3844

Fax: 602-404-2986

Email: info@casago.com

Wishing you success!

ABOUT THE AUTHOR

Steve Schwab is the Founder and Chief Executive Officer of the Schwab Organization, the parent company of Casago. He has been in the vacation rental business since graduating from New Mexico State University; over 15 years.

As a former member of the U.S. Army Special Operations community, Steve has a unique understanding of what it takes to establish delivery systems that are goal focused. For the vacation rental property management industry this means putting the right people and processes in place to ensure that all of an owner's needs are met in a timely, transparent, and exceptional manner.

Steve is a pioneer in performance driven industry software. His position as managing partner in Streamline Vacation Rental Software has allowed him to create many industry "first" technologies that continue to change the market. His creative work has been featured in numerous publications and television appearances.

However, his commitment to excellence doesn't stop with technology. It is a value that is instilled in everyone who works with and for the organization. Steve's emphasis on ethics and world class performance has been exemplified in exclusive resorts and estates in ten cities and two countries.

Steve is always looking for others who share his values and interest in providing stellar property management.

You may contact Steve at:
steve@casago.com

APPENDIX A
Minimum Recommended Furnishings
and Accessories

<u>Kitchen</u>

Baking Dish
Blender
Cake Pan
Can Opener
Cheese Grater
Coffee Mugs
Coffee Maker (Auto Shut Off)
Colander
Cookie Sheets
Cooking Tools – Ladle, Spatula, Spoon, etc.
Cookware Set – Stainless Steel Preferred
Corkscrew Cutting Board (2)
Dinnerware – Designer Line
       1 BR – Service for 4
       2 BR – Service for 8
       3 BR – Service for 12
       4 BR – Service for 16
       5 BR – Service for 18
Fire Extinguisher
Flatware – Best Quality
       1 BR – Service for 4
       2 BR – Service for 8
       3 BR – Service for 12

4 BR – Service for 16
5 BR – Service for 18

Food Storage Containers – Bowls & Lids
Glassware
1 BR – Service for 4
2 BR – Service for 8 including:
Stemmed Glasses
Drinking Glasses
Beverage / Rocks
Plastic cups for pool area
Ice Cream Scoop
Kitchen Knife Set/Block or assorted
Measuring Cups & Spoons
Microwave Oven
Mixing Bowls
Serving Platters and Bowls
Steak Knife Set
Tea Kettle
Toaster / Toaster Oven
Wastebasket
Labeled Recycle Basket if applicable
Decorative pieces
Salt & Pepper Shaker/Grinder
10 to 14-Piece cookware set (pots and pans)
Upgrades: Wok, Pizza stone/pan, pasta boiler, water filter & other miscellaneous gourmet kitchen supplies would be listed as Gourmet Kitchen on our web page.

Linens

3 sets of linens for each bed, 200-300 plus count

1 blanket, comforter & bead skirt for each bed Shams for each pillow
Extra Pillows
3 Towel sets for each prospective guest
1 pool towel for each prospective guest
4+ Dish Cloths and Dish Towels
2+ Pot Holders
Placemat & Cloth Napkin for each dining table seat

Bathrooms

Bath Set for each bathroom including:
Bath Rugs
Shower Curtain
Soap Dish
Toothbrush Holder
Toilet Brush and Holder
Waste Basket
Hair Dryer

Miscellaneous

Voice Mail or Answering Machine
Alarm Clock
BBQ & Utensils; Minimum 4 burner Gas Grill
Broom & Dust Pan
Cleaning Supplies: Mop, dust rags, polish, cleaners, etc.
Coasters
Extra Ice Trays
Flashlight

Garden Hose, Hanger and spray nozzle
Clothes Hangers (Platinum Homes should have wooden not plastic hangers)
Iron (Auto Shut Off) & Full Size Ironing Board Laundry Baskets
Spare Light Bulbs
Mop
Paper Towel Holder
Patio Furniture and Loungers (Avoid Patio Tables with Glass tops)
Plunger
Reading Lamps
Stereo with CD + iPod/MP3 Player Connection
2+ Telephones – 1 Cordless
Flat Screen Televisions: 40" or larger for main living area and recommend 22" or larger TV's for each bedroom.
DVD/BluRay – Minimum 1 for main TV & one for Master Suite
Hi-Speed Internet Connection (Wired/Wireless) Homes with pools should have a Skimmer and a Brush
Smoke Detectors
10 Piece Tool Set
Garage Ladder (Tall enough to reach the highest light bulb/smoke detector in your house)
Ice Chest/Cooler

This recommended furnishings list is the minimum we think the home should have.

87359945R00091

Made in the USA
San Bernardino, CA
03 September 2018